Ben's book

Illustrated by Nina O'Connell

Nelson

Hide and seek

"We will play hide and seek,"
said Ben.

Jip is up the tree.

Deb is in the pot.

Ben looks for Jip and Deb.

He looks and looks.

"I can see Jip,"

said Ben.

"But I can't see Deb."

"Here I am," said Deb.

"I am in the pot."

The big box

"I like this big box,"
said Ben the dog.
"I will sit in it."

"I like this big box,"
said Sam the fox.
"I will sit in it."

"I like this big box,"
said Pat the pig.
"I will sit on it."

"Have you seen Ben?
Have you seen Sam?"
said Meg.

"I have not seen them,"
said Pat.
"I can see them," said Meg.

Bad Ben

"Have you seen my hat, Ben?
You are a bad dog,"
said Deb.

12

"Have you seen my shoe, Ben?
You are a bad dog,"
said Meg.

"Have you seen my socks, Ben?
You are a bad dog,"
said Jip.

"Have you seen Ben?"
said Pat.

"Ben is a bad dog.

He has gone to bed,"

said Meg, Jip and Deb.

16